Ten Kids and a Pup

By Debbie Croft

Ten kids went to look
at a pup.

Dad said Kim
can get the pup.

"No!" said Nat.

"Let me get the pup!"

"Mum, can we get the pup?"
said Win and Sal.

Mum said Win and Sal
can get the pup!

But Val, Min and Meg
look at the pup.

And Rob, Liv and Jon
look, too.

"Ten kids and a pup!"
said Sal to Win and Mum.

Mum got her big red hat.

In the hat went ...
Kim, Nat, Win, Sal,
Val, Min, Meg,
Rob, Liv and Jon.

Mum got Kim!

"Kim wins the pup!"
said Mum.

CHECKING FOR MEANING

1. How many kids went to look at the pup? *(Literal)*

2. Who got the pup? *(Literal)*

3. How do you think the other kids felt when Kim's name was pulled out of the hat? *(Inferential)*

EXTENDING VOCABULARY

went	Look at the word *went*. How many letters are in this word? How many sounds are there?
Win and **Min**	*Win* and *Min* is another pair of rhyming names in the book. What other words do you know that rhyme with *Win* and *Min*?
Val	Find a name in the book that rhymes with *Val*. Which letter changes to make the new name? Which letters stay the same?

MOVING BEYOND THE TEXT

1. What are some different places that you can get a pet from?

2. What do you think happened when Kim got the pup home?

3. What are some things you need to do to take care of a dog?

4. When have you won something? How did you feel?

SPEED SOUNDS

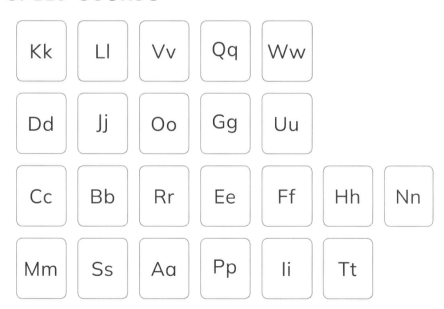

Kk	Ll	Vv	Qq	Ww		
Dd	Jj	Oo	Gg	Uu		
Cc	Bb	Rr	Ee	Ff	Hh	Nn
Mm	Ss	Aa	Pp	Ii	Tt	

PRACTICE WORDS

Win

Kim

Sal

Let

Val

Liv

kids

wins